Stories

FROM THE

Wilderness

A STUDY OF THE ISRAELITES' JOURNEY FROM EGYPT TO THE PROMISED LAND

By
Erin H. Warren

feasting on truth

For Lynda
Your love of the Word is contagious, and this study exists in part because of the countless mornings spent across the table from one another studying Scripture together. You showed me how to find God in His Word. I'm forever grateful.

He makes a road through a sea.
He brings water from rocks and bread from heaven.
He makes slaves victorious against warriors.
He makes a way for holiness to dwell in the midst of unholiness.
He loves even when rejected.
He forgives over and over and over again.
Who does that?

"I have said these things to you, that in me you may have peace. In the world you will have tribulation.
But take heart; I have overcome the world." – John 16:33

contents

start here

I sat down in the salon swivel chair, excited to finally get a haircut. I mean, haircut days are the best days, am I right?! And I was long overdue. This was my first time meeting my new hair stylist, and she had come highly recommended. As she began talking with me about my hair and prepping to wash it, she tilted her head, and her face turned. "Your hair is dead," she said. Trying to hide my shock, I played it off and kept talking in that nervous, chatty way. I had been growing my hair out and only wanted a small trim. But my hair was dead. This wouldn't be a small trim. It wasn't until I was back in the car, taking that post-haircut selfie, that I realized she had cut off over four inches. I started crying.

The dead hair was just a symbol of how I felt inside. I felt lifeless, like I was living in the valley of dry bones from Ezekiel 37. My family was in the middle of a wilderness season, and even my hair was feeling the effects.

Maybe you've been there. Maybe you're there right now . . . the place that feels stalled, like life is passing you by; like everyone else in the world is moving forward, and you are stuck walking in circles. You can't take any more bad news. Everything around you feels lifeless. Your dreams are dead. Your future is uncertain. Your pain feels crushing.

Merriam-Webster Dictionary defines *wilderness* as "an empty or pathless area or region." [1] The wilderness is uncharted territory. It's the place where we feel lost, not knowing where to go, because there is no path to follow. It's a place we see often in Scripture. There's a thread throughout the whole Bible centered around the wilderness, and it starts right in the first chapter of Genesis.

Now the earth was formless and empty, darkness was over the surface of the
deep, and the Spirit of God was hovering over the waters.
Genesis 1:2 (NIV)

---

1 "Wilderness." *Merriam-Webster.com Dictionary*, Merriam-Webster, https://www.merriam-webster.com/dictionary/wilderness. Accessed 20 Aug. 2021.

The Hebrew word for *formless* comes from a root word meaning "to lie waste; a desolation (of surface), i.e. Desert; figuratively, a worthless thing; adverbially, in vain—confusion, empty place, without form, nothing, (thing of) nought, vain, vanity, waste, wilderness." [2] Before the creation of this world, God calls it a wilderness. But while we see a place that is worthless, a waste, confusing, chaotic, and empty, God sees a place to display His glory. And time and time again throughout Scripture, God takes the worthless, seemingly wasteful, confusing, chaotic, and empty places and uses them as a backdrop to prove His character, draw us in, and display His glory.

The first place in Scripture we often think of when we hear the word wilderness is in Exodus. It's a story many of us are familiar with. God's people, the Israelites, are enslaved in Egypt. God sends Moses to Pharaoh saying, "Let my people go," and after a series of plagues, Pharaoh relents. The Israelites leave Egypt bound for the Promised Land, but first they must go through the wilderness.

The journey from Egypt to Canaan (the Promised Land) is about an eleven-day journey. *Eleven days!* But instead, the people of God wander for *forty years* through desert. Growing up, I remember thinking, *Goodness. If they had just obeyed, they could have skipped the wilderness part and gone straight to the Promised Land!* I saw the wilderness as a punishment for disobedience, a punishment that could have been avoided. As we will see in this study, yes, there is an element of truth to that statement, but there was a key truth that I missed: God *purposely* led them into the wilderness in the first place.

God often leads by way of wandering. He does not take us on the most direct route. He leads in places that feel aimless and empty, because there are some lessons about God that can only be learned in the fertile soil of the wilderness.

But this story is not just hope for us during hard seasons of life; it's a picture of this life altogether. We refer to it as the "already but not yet." Just as the Israelites were saved from slavery, we have been redeemed from our slavery to sin, but we are not in the Promised Land of Heaven yet. We are wandering the wilderness of life in between. Life on earth brings hurt, division, pride, fear, and more. It often leaves us with questions about who God is. But our God has not left us here as orphans.

Every time I read our theme verse for this study, I want to cry. It feels so personal:

> *For the LORD your God has blessed you in all the work of your hands. He knows your going through this great wilderness. These forty years the LORD your God has been with you. You have lacked nothing.*
> *Deuteronomy 2:7*

To be honest, the first time I read it, I thought there was a typo. The grammar nerd in me thought, *"your" needs to be "you are."* In fact, even my graphic designer corrected it to "you're" in the first draft of the cover. Every time I type it, my computer underlines it with a little red line, as if to say, "Classic you're/your mistake here!" But, come to find out, it's not a typo. There's a difference between "He knows you are going through this great wilderness" and "He knows your going . . ." The first is passive. He knows you are going through a great wilderness. He knows about it. But the second, the correct one, is intimate. He knows *your* going. His eyes are on you at all times. He is El Roi, the God who sees you, even when walking through desolate, seemingly lifeless places.

Several other translations put it this way: "He has watched over your journey" (NIV), "He has

---

2   Strong's Hebrew: 8414. Tohu. *BibleHub.com*, biblehub.com/hebrew/8414.htm.

6

watched your every step" (NLT), "He has known your wandering" (NASB), "He knows your trudging" (NKJV). His eyes have not missed one thing. There is not one step you've taken, one room you've walked into, one phone call, one doctor visit, one tear that has spilled over, one plea for help, or one prayer for provision that He has missed. He has seen it all. Your LORD God—Yahweh, the One True God—has never left your side. He goes before you. He goes with you. He goes behind you. He hems you in. His hand is on you (Deuteronomy 31:8, Psalm 139:5). And because of that, because El Shaddai, God Almighty, sees you and goes with you, you have lacked nothing. And that is what we are going to see throughout the next eleven weeks. We are going to see who God is in the wilderness, in our wandering, in the desolate, lifeless, chaotic, seemingly worthless and aimless places of our life.

The God of the Promised Land is the same God in the wilderness.

WHY STUDY INDUCTIVELY?

I classify this study as a Guided Inductive Bible Study because it is designed to give you a foundation and walk you through the inductive study process. When I first heard of inductive study, I was pretty intimidated. But, it's just a fancy term for studying with your own heart and mind first. I honestly didn't even know I *could* study this way until a few years ago at a conference. I had the privilege of hearing one of my favorite Bible teachers speak, and the following quote from her talk forever changed the way I look at Bible study:

> *We cannot be content being curators of other people's opinions about a book we can't be bothered to read ourselves.* — Jen Wilkin

I realized my entire Christian life I had been a librarian, curating other people's thoughts and beliefs and study findings. It became my driving passion to not only read and study Scripture for myself, but to help other women do the same.

I'm so glad you're here! My prayer is that this book helps you:

- Release the bonds of a "perfect quiet time" to find deeper, richer time in the Word
- Build confidence as you learn how to study the Bible firsthand
- Discover truths about God and His character
- Grow in your faith and knowledge in a way that produces life change

HOW TO USE THIS STUDY

The story of the Israelites' journey through the wilderness is a unique story because it spans several books in various pieces and parts. Typically, I love (and encourage women) to study whole books of Scripture at a time, but I want to study the narrative of this story through the wilderness as a whole so we can see the big picture of who God is as He leads His people. This study highlights some of the major events that take places between Egypt and the Promised Land.

I have learned so many deep truths about God's character and who He is in my wilderness places. I am so excited you are taking this journey too. I pray that these truths will encourage you in your own wilderness places.

For each week of study, you will have two to three stories to read. For each story, you will find space to answer four simple questions (see pages 11–14 for more on this), as well as some additional study questions to help get you started. Each week also includes blank pages for you to add your own study notes, a response page, and space for teaching and small group notes.

Before your first meeting, take some time to answer the context questions on page 22. Context is crucial when studying Scripture. While this ancient book has not changed and is relevant for us today, we must remember it was written during a different time period and to different people groups. Understanding the cultural context is key to interpreting Scripture. Answering these questions and keeping them at the forefront of your mind as you study will help you better understand what you are reading.

One of the most life changing aspects of Bible study for me has been asking the question, "What does this say about God?" as I am studying. This is not a book about us; and particularly in the wilderness, we learn so much about who God is when we ask that question. With each passage you study, you have space to record the names and characteristics of God from that passage. (See pages 17–19 for more information on this.) At the end of each study week, there is a page to record a prayer to God as well as a fill-in-the-blank sentence to help you take His character and apply it to your own life. When we view our life and our circumstances through the lens of His character, we will see lasting change.

The teaching for this Bible study is available on Season 5 of the Feasting on Truth podcast and on YouTube (www.youtube.com/c/erinhwarren). For more information on this study, go to FeastingOnTruth.com/Wilderness.

Here are some more tips to help you as you study:

Move Slowly
Many Bible studies plow through Scripture, covering a chapter (or sometimes more) a day. There's certainly a time and a place for that, but I've found when I move through Scripture slowly, reading small sections or focusing on one aspect of the study over the course of one week, the Word of God soaks into my heart and mind deeply. I remember it more easily. I memorize it more effectively. What I love about this particular way of studying is that if I feel the need to stop and let a particular verse sink in, I can do so without feeling like I'm falling behind. It also leaves room for the Holy Spirit to do what only He can do. Which leads me to . . .

Let the Holy Spirit Guide You
Jesus gives us this promise in John 14:26: "But the Helper, the Holy Spirit, whom the Father will send in my name, he will teach you all things and bring to your remembrance all that I have said to you." Anytime I sit down to study, I start with prayer. I ask the Holy Spirit to teach me all the things and to help me remember all the things. That's His job. He's there to help, so invite Him into your time.

Take the Pressure Off
Our time with the Lord doesn't have to be this picture-perfect composition of Bible, notebook, and a cup of coffee (oh how I do love me some good coffee though). The words "quiet time" are not in the Bible, and I've found one size does not fit all. Our time in the Word will change with our stage of life. I tend to deep-dive study about twice a week, but I meditate on it every day. You may sit down and do all of your study in one day or you may devote an hour a day. Find what works for you and stick with it!

Don't Do This Alone

Some of my deepest relationships are ones built on the Word. They are women who gathered around a table or in a living room or online, and we had hard conversations with the Word of Truth between us. Invite a few girlfriends to do this with you. I even included a fun recipe in the back of the book you can make when you get together!

I recommend completing all of the homework on your own before listening to the teaching for the week. You can either listen on your own time or watch together with your group.

Finding time is hard. Women often tell me that they need to put their families first, that work is too crazy, or that they just don't have time to get together with other women for Bible study. Can I challenge you a bit? Is there any time more well spent than investing in our relationship with God? It's hard to pour out from an empty cup. We need to be constantly filled with Jesus, so we can pour out Jesus to our friends, family, and to God. Yes, this may look different in different seasons of life, but you won't regret making it a priority to spend time in the Word with other women.

A LITTLE BACKGROUND INFORMATION

The first five books of the Bible are known as The Torah in Hebrew (Pentateuch in Greek) or The Books of Law. They were written by Moses in the wilderness, and the purpose was to tell the people of Israel their story. As they were preparing to enter the Promised Land, these stories, poems, laws, and genealogies told them not only who they were and where they came from, but also taught them who their God was. These books taught them His name and His character.

For this study, we will read through passages in Exodus, Numbers, Deuteronomy, and Joshua and move with the Israelites from Egypt into the land of Canaan. Technically, we are jumping into the middle of the story of God's people, so it's helpful to also understand the Scriptural context of the wilderness story.

The book of Genesis closes with the story of Joseph in Egypt. Joseph, sold into slavery by his jealous brothers, spends years facing trouble and hardship before rising to second-in-command in all of Egypt. It's the stuff of Hollywood movies—famine spreads across the land and Joseph's brothers, desperate for food, go to Egypt for help. What ensues is a reunion for the ages. The book ends with God graciously providing for His people through the wisdom of Joseph, and all of his father Jacob's household moves to Egypt and is saved.

The book of Exodus begins with God's people growing in great number while in Egypt. They increase and multiply at such an alarming rate, Pharaoh makes them slaves for fear of an uprising. He makes several proclamations in hopes of keeping the people of God down. But God raises up an unlikely leader: Moses. It's a remarkable story, and I encourage you to skim through Exodus 1–11 before we start this study. This will help refresh your memory about Moses and the people of God as we begin to study their incredible journey.

COMPANION TEACHINGS AND OTHER RESOURCES

I am committed to walking alongside you as you study Scripture inductively. I know you can do this, and I want to help you be successful. I have personally curated and put together a valuable study resource for you called *The Alongside Guide*. Each week, you'll receive an email from me with helpful insight, links to that week's teaching video and podcast, study notes with cross-references, quotes,

characteristics of God, small group discussion questions, and more. It's everything you need to be successful in your study, and it gets delivered right to your inbox. Scan the QR code or visit FeastingOnTruth.com/Wilderness to sign up.

LET'S FEAST!
Eugene Peterson wrote a book titled *A Long Obedience in the Same Direction*. I love that title, and I think it perfectly captures what walking through the wilderness, the in-between, the already-but-not-yet looks like. We likely won't often see overnight life change or radical transformations, but instead a slow, steady plodding. It's taking step after step, minute by minute, hour by hour, day by day, year after year in the direction our God leads. It is my prayer we will do just that.

I pray this study emboldens your steps, reveals the truth of who God is, and encourages you to keep walking, even through the hard seasons of your life. I can't wait to take this journey with you!

Because of Christ,

Erin H. Warren

four simple questions

Good Bible study is rooted in asking the right questions of Scripture. While this study gives you some specific questions to answer, you can begin to go deeper into understanding the passage by asking four simple questions. Our first inclination is to ask, "What does this mean to me?" We want to cut right to the ending. Instead, learning to first understand the context, summary, and character of God in the passage will help us better discern the meaning and our response. I have adopted what I call *Four Simple Questions* as the foundation of my time in the Word. Yes, this takes a little more time and effort, but the practice of persevering through the Word is a valuable one. These four simple questions, as well as other helpful tips and resources for inductive study, are further explained in my book, *Feasting on Truth: Savor the Life-giving Word of God.*

START WITH CONTEXT

It's important to remember that while the Bible was written for us and is applicable to our lives today (Hebrews 4:12), we are not the original audience. It is a book not written in modern America, but in the ancient Middle East. If we do not first answer some key questions to understand the context, we cannot properly understand the passage and its intent. Most of these answers can be found in a good study Bible.

FOUR SIMPLE QUESTIONS

I realized that one of my downfalls when attempting to read and study the Bible for myself was not knowing which questions to ask. Many of the methods I tried were either too open or too rigid. Asking four simple questions provided the right balance of structure and flexibility I needed. I want to release you from thinking this has to look a certain way—it doesn't. Basically: Are you showing up? Are you changing? Are you connected? Does that make you want to keep showing up? If you answer yes to all of these, then you're on the right track! Here is a brief overview of each question:

11

1. **What does this say?**

   Before we can interpret Scripture, we need to know what's going on in the passage. Some methods would call this *observation* or the *aim of the passage*.

   - Write a 1–2 sentence summary of what the passage is about—no interpretation, just the facts.

   - Answer the questions: Who? What? Where? When?

   - Are there any repeated words or phrases?

   - Are there any transitional words (therefore, so, but, and, etc.)? Remember, every word is there for a reason.

2. **What does this say about God?**

   This to me has been the most transformative question to ask during Bible study. This book is not about us; it's about God. His character and name are written on every page. Before we can understand our response, we must know who He is.

   - What names of God are used? (His names speak to His character.)

   - What characteristics of God are in this passage?

   - I include Jesus in this as well: What does this passage tell us about Jesus?

   - You can find lists of the names and characteristics of God on pages 18–19.

   - Each week, complete the sentence "Because God is _____, I can _____."

3. **What does this mean?**

   PRAY. PRAY. PRAY. Ask the Holy Spirit to guide you in this. Using context, the summary, and other observations you have made, begin to be a detective. Remember the lens through which you are looking. Yes, this takes work, but it's worth doing!

   - Read the passage in multiple translations. What differences do you see?

   - Look up words in the English dictionary.

   - What other passages in Scripture are related to this one? (These are called cross-references.)

   - Read a trusted commentary or study Bible.

   - Research the original language (the Old Testament was originally written in Hebrew and the New Testament in Greek).

   - Go to FeastingOnTruth.com/Resources for recommended resources, Bibles, and commentaries.

4. **How should I respond?**

   Our Bible study should change us. John 17:17 says, "Sanctify them in the truth; your word is truth." *Sanctify* is a big churchy word that means "to purify or to make holy." It's the act of separating ourselves from the actions of our flesh and dedicating more of our lives and actions to God. God's Word has a purpose in our lives (Isaiah 55:10–11), and we shouldn't stop at knowing its meaning. Instead, we should respond:

   - Is there an action I need to take?

- A conversation I need to have?
- A moment of worship?
- Something I should let go?
- Write out a prayer.

However you feel led to respond, write it down and enlist someone to hold you accountable.

OTHER HELPFUL TIPS

Listen to the Passage
Use a Bible app to listen to the passages each week. We often feel like this is a cop-out, but for thousands of years, the Word of God was passed down orally from generation to generation. It's a book meant to be read out loud, and when you listen to it, you'll be amazed at how much you pick up on that you didn't notice when reading it.

Use Different Colored Pens
I've found using different colored pens when writing my study notes helps me remember where the note came from. For instance, I use different colors for rewriting the Scripture verses, my thoughts, certain study Bibles, cross-references or different translations, commentary quotes, and Greek or Hebrew word definitions. I don't really have a color system, so the colors change from time to time. That's okay too!

Start with a Clean Copy of God's Word
A study Bible adds additional commentary. Using a Bible that doesn't have any additional commentary removes the temptation to peek at notes before fully understanding the passage on your own. If you do not have a non-study Bible, don't fret! You can print out chapters on several Bible websites including www.BibleGateway.com. I use an ESV journaling Bible for my initial study (which has very few footnotes), then move to other versions and other study Bibles as I go through my study week. Speaking of translations . . .

A Note About Translations
There are a myriad of translations out there, so how do you know which to pick? First, it's important to know where translations come from. The Old Testament was originally written in Hebrew, while the New Testament was written in Greek (though a few portions were written in Aramaic).

Over the years, translators have used original copies written in these languages to interpret Scripture into English (and other languages as well). Translations fall on a spectrum between two ends: word-for-word (translations that use the closest English word to the original word) and thought-for-thought (translations that rephrase the words into more modern, understandable English). Technically, all of them are a mix of the two, but some lean more toward one end or the other.

Some examples of translations that lean toward word-for-word include: English Standard Version (ESV—my top choice), New American Standard Bible (NAS or NASB), and King James Version (KJV). These are the closest to the original language, but we can sometimes miss the cultural context.

An example of thought-for-thought is the New Living Translation (NLT).

There are also versions that are more toward the middle of the spectrum, such as the Christian Standard Bible (CSB) and the New International Version (NIV).

The last kind of translation is not necessarily a translation at all, but rather a paraphrase. Paraphrase Bibles, like *The Message*, should be treated more like commentary because, while they can bring insight into the meaning of the passage, they are not Scripture themselves. I rarely use this type. If you do use a paraphrase, wait until you've completed questions 1–3 and are consulting other commentaries for additional insights.

Welcome to the Feast!

See? Simple. Yes, it takes practice, but honestly, it doesn't take as long as you'd think. You just have to be willing to spend time with Jesus. In Acts 4, Peter and John are on trial before the religious leaders (the smartest of the smart when it came to the Law), and in verse 13 it says, "Now when they saw the boldness of Peter and John, and perceived that they were uneducated, common men, they were astonished. And they recognized that they had been with Jesus." Uneducated. Common. Peter and John hadn't been to seminary, but they had been *with* Jesus.

What I've found is that there is not one method that will make all of this work for you. The power is not in the method. The power is in the Word of God. The power is in spending time with Jesus in the Word with the Holy Spirit as your guide.

When you see your life change and you find community around the Word, you will find yourself returning to Scripture, growing more confident as you study, and discovering the joy and excitement of Feasting on Truth.

Visit FeastingOnTruth.com/HowTo for more information
and in-depth teachings on these questions.

small group guide

I am a firm believer in gathering together around the Word of God. It is at the heart of Feasting on Truth. As stated in *start here*, I believe that small group discussion is incredibly important when studying the Bible. I heard a pastor say, "Our time in the Word should be personal but never private." I do not believe we are called to study in isolation, and I believe it is in those places of isolation where Satan loves to tempt us. Discussing the passage in a small group setting (even if it's with only one other woman) helps confirm what the Holy Spirit taught you. It holds us accountable to truth. Not only that, but I learn so much from other women too. They will see truths within those passages that I miss. It helps build layers of understanding.

Leading a group is not nearly as difficult as it seems. I like to think of group leaders more like discussion leaders. A great discussion leader talks less than a third of the group time. You may need to speak first or jump in to get the conversation going, but the goal is to get the group talking.

Teaching for each chapter is available on Season 5 of the Feasting on Truth podcast or my YouTube channel: YouTube.com/c/erinhwarren.

Here are some other tips and a guide for your small group time:

Lead with authenticity
You do not have to have all the answers or have it all together to lead. I do not have it all together, and I fail miserably every day at doing what I know I should (Romans 7!). But I don't have to air all my dirty laundry to be authentic, and I never want my authenticity to enable sin in other people's lives. I've found that when I'm real about where I am and I invite women in to see how God is working on me in those areas, it invites them into authentic life change as well.

Set up a group text or use a group chat app
Connection throughout the week is key to building connection within your group. If you are not tech savvy or keeping up with a group chat isn't your strength, ask someone in the group to take charge of that. It's a great way to get others involved too! Throughout the week, you can check in on your group or share a verse or a particular insight into the passage.

Start with an ice breaker question
It doesn't have to be deep or spiritual, just something to get the conversation flowing. These types of questions are always a great way to help a group of women get to know each other.

15

Share your summary

Have the women share their summary for that week's passage. Depending on the size of your group, you may want to limit this to two to three women.

Ask: What characteristics of God did you see in this week's passage?

This works well "popcorn style." Let the women jump in with various names and characteristics of God and the verses that correspond. I usually add these to my own notes as well.

Use the weekly discussion questions

There are discussion questions marked within each week's homework. For additional weekly discussion questions, go to FeastingOnTruth.com/Dwell and sign up to receive *The Alongside Guide* in your email. Each week, you'll get additional questions (as well as other resources and notes) delivered right to your inbox.

Share "Because God is" statements

This is a simple one, and I love it when everyone shares theirs! Depending on how long you have been together, some women in your group may not feel comfortable sharing the nitty-gritty of their lives. Having everyone share their "Because God is" statement is a way to engage the women who do not feel comfortable speaking up.

Share prayer requests

Sharing what is going on in our lives opens the door to build community and meet needs. I'll never forget sitting in a group when a woman shared that she needed prayer that she could pass her driving test. Across the table, another woman in the group spoke up and said, "I can help you learn to drive!" A couple months later, I received a picture of the two women holding a brand-new driver's license. It was incredible! Praying for one another is commanded, so allow time for this with your group. Pray with one another. Pray throughout the week. When we do this, we get to share an inheritance in what God is doing through the lives of others.

GROUP LIST

NAME	PHONE	EMAIL

16

knowing God

For too many years, I struggled with knowing how to interpret Scripture and apply these ancient words to my life. I did not know that God promises to equip us in studying Scripture through the Holy Spirit. And truthfully, I treated my Bible like one of those balls you shake, ask a question, flip over, and find your answer. Too many times I came to Scripture looking for an answer to my question, or I treated it like a yearbook—looking for all the pictures of myself.

Then, I began asking a different question, and my entire Bible study and life changed. I asked, "What does this say about God?" This shifted my perspective from a self-centered approach toward Scripture (where I am always asking, "What does this mean *to* me or *for* me?") to a God-centered approach—intentionally looking for and seeking out what each passage teaches me about God.

The Bible is not about me. It is first and foremost a book about God, and His name and character are written across every page. Our purpose on earth is to know God and make Him known, to love God and love others. But we can't love what we don't know; we can't worship what we don't know. And the primary way we know God is through His Word. The pursuit of knowledge about God is not optional; it's essential.

On the following pages, you will find two lists to help you: Names of God and Characteristics of God. It's not comprehensive, and there are spaces for you to add others as you discover more with each passage you read. Here are ways you can have a God-centered approach to your study:

- Ask, "What characteristics of God do I see in this passage?"

- Ask, "What names of God do I see in this passage?" (His names speak to His character.)

- Complete this sentence: Because God is _____, I can _____.

I understand there are different roles of the Trinity (God the Father, God the Son, God the Holy Spirit), but for the sake of simplicity (and especially as you are beginning), I think of them as One. If you need further help, visit www.FeastingOnTruth.com for more information and resources.

17

names of God

Abba Father

Adonai *(Lord, Master)*

Alpha and Omega

Bread of Life

Chief Cornerstone

Creator

Deliverer

El Elyon *(The Most High God)*

El Olam *(The Everlasting God)*

El Roi *(The God Who Sees Me)*

El Shaddai *(The Lord God Almighty)*

Elohim

Emmanuel

Everlasting Father

Great High Priest

Holy One

I AM

King of Kings

Lamb of God

Light of the World

Lion of Judah

Lord of Lords

Mighty God

Morning Star

Prince of Peace

Resurrection and the Life

Savior

Wonderful Counselor

Yahweh Amen *(The Lord is Truth)*

Yahweh Jireh *(The Lord Provides)*

Yahweh Nissi *(The Lord is my Banner)*

Yahweh-Raah *(The Lord is my Shepherd)*

Yahweh Rapha *(The Lord Heals)*

Yahweh Shalom *(The Lord is Peace)*

18

characteristics of God

Abounding in Steadfast Love

Compassionate

Deliberate

Faithful

Forgiving

Full of Grace

Good

Glorious

Gracious

Guide

Holy

Immutable *(Unchanging)*

Infinite

Invisible

Jealous

Just

Kind

Long-Suffering/Patient

Love

Merciful

Mighty

Omnipotent *(All-Powerful)*

Omnipresent

Omniscient *(All-Knowing)*

One

Perfect

Protector

Provider

Refuge/Help

Righteous

Self-Sufficient

Slow to Anger

Sovereign

Trustworthy

Truth

Wise

With Us

MAP OF ISRAELITES' JOURNEY FROM EGYPT TO THE PROMISED LAND

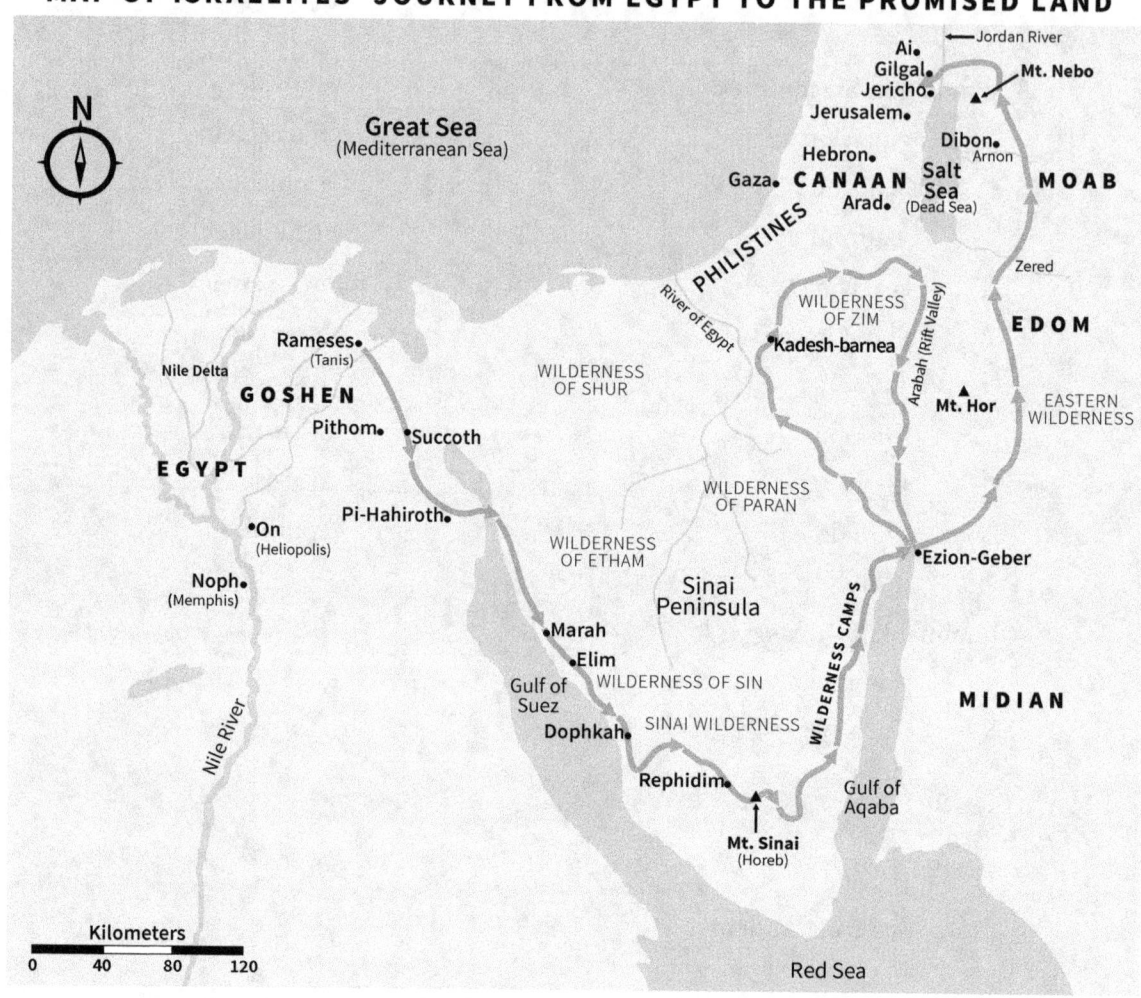

Stories from the Wilderness

CONTEXT

Stories
FROM THE
Wilderness
CONTEXT NOTES

Who wrote the first five books of the Bible?
What do you know about this author?

To whom were these books written?
When were they written?
What is the genre of these books?
What was the intent or purpose?

What was going on in history when they were written?

Stories FROM THE Wilderness

CONTEXT NOTES

Stories
FROM THE
Wilderness
CONTEXT NOTES

24

Stories FROM THE Wilderness

TEACHING NOTES

Stories from the Wilderness

WEEK 1

EXODUS 12
EXODUS 13

READ EXODUS 12

WHAT DOES THIS SAY?

Write a 2–3 sentence summary of this passage.

Who? What? Where? When?

List any repeated words or phrases.

List any transitional words.

WHAT DOES THIS SAY ABOUT GOD?

What characteristics of God do you see in this passage?

WHAT DOES THIS MEAN?

The Passover (vv. 1–28, 43–51)

Describe in detail what the Lord told the Israelites to do to save them from the tenth plague.

How often were they commanded to celebrate this feast? Why?

How is the Passover a picture of Jesus? (See Mark 14:12; John 1:29; John 19:28–37; Romans 5:11; 1 Corinthians 5:7; Hebrews 4:15; Hebrews 9:14, 18–22; 1 Peter 1:19.)

The Exodus (vv. 29–42)
List everything the Israelites took with them out of Egypt.

How many Israelites were there?

Why was the bread unleavened?

How long had the Israelites been in Egypt? What is significant about the day they left?

DISCUSSION: Why were the Israelites able to leave with so much? What does this tell us about God's ability to provide for His people? (v. 36)

READ EXODUS 13

WHAT DOES THIS SAY?

Write a 2–3 sentence summary of this passage.

Who? What? Where? When?

List any repeated words or phrases.

List any transitional words.

WHAT DOES THIS SAY ABOUT GOD?

What characteristics of God do you see in this passage?

WHAT DOES THIS MEAN?

The Feast of Unleavened Bread (vv. 1–16)

What did Moses command the people to do in v. 3?

List all of the inhabitants of Canaan.

In what ways were they to memorialize the exodus out of Egypt?

DISCUSSION: What does this tell us about the importance of remembering what God has done?

Pillars of Cloud and Fire (vv. 17–22)

Why did God not lead the Israelites on the fastest route?

DISCUSSION: Look back on your life. Have you seen God purposely lead you into a wilderness season? Why do you think He may have led you there?

How did God guide His people? Why?

Think about a desert. Why do you think a cloud during the daytime and a fire at night would be beneficial to the Israelites?

Stories FROM THE Wilderness

WEEK 1 NOTES

Stories FROM THE Wilderness

WEEK 1 NOTES

36

Stories FROM THE Wilderness

WEEK 1 NOTES

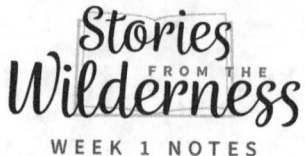
HOW SHOULD I RESPOND?

God led the Israelites into the wilderness, but He also went with them and guided them. How does He still do this for us today? How can you actively trust His character in your wilderness places?

Write a prayer praising God for who He is in this passage.

Because God is:

      I can:

Stories FROM THE Wilderness

TEACHING NOTES

Stories
FROM THE
Wilderness

TEACHING NOTES

Stories FROM THE Wilderness

GROUP NOTES

Stories FROM THE Wilderness

WEEK 2

EXODUS 14
EXODUS 15

READ EXODUS 14

WHAT DOES THIS SAY?

Write a 2–3 sentence summary of this passage.

Who? What? Where? When?

List any repeated words or phrases.

List any transitional words.

WHAT DOES THIS SAY ABOUT GOD?

What characteristics of God do you see in this passage?

WHAT DOES THIS MEAN?

Crossing the Red Sea (vv. 1–31)

Where does God tell the Israelites to encamp? Which way are they facing? (Look in the ESV version.)

How many chariots did Pharaoh take? Horses? Horeseman?

How were the Israelites exiting Egypt according to v. 8? Why do you think they had this confidence?

How did the Israelites shift their gaze? What did they see? (v. 10) What was their reaction? (vv. 11–12)

DISCUSSION: God told the Israelites to camp with their back toward the enemy. Why do you think He did that? What does this tell us about which way to look in our own lives today?

What does Moses say to the people in vv. 13–14?

What does God say to the people in v. 15? What would have been forward?

DISCUSSION: Verse 14 is often quoted to bring comfort to someone fighting a battle in their life. How would you interpret this verse reading in context of vv. 13–16?

What happens in vv. 19–20? Can Israel see their enemy now? Now where would they have to look? How does God do this for us today?

How did the Red Sea split? Why do you think this is important?

What does the Lord do in v. 24? What is the reaction of the Egyptians?

How are the Israelites changed by this experience? (v. 31)

Read Matthew 14:22–33. What similarities do you see in this story compared to the crossing of the Red Sea?

What caused Peter to sink?

Write out Hebrews 2:1. How can we keep our eyes focused on God and not on our fears?

Stories FROM THE Wilderness

WEEK 2 NOTES

READ EXODUS 15

WHAT DOES THIS SAY?

Write a 2–3 sentence summary of this passage.

Who? What? Where? When?

List any repeated words or phrases.

List any transitional words.

WHAT DOES THIS SAY ABOUT GOD?

What characteristics of God do you see in this passage?

WHAT DOES THIS MEAN?

Song of Moses (vv. 1–21)

Who is singing this song?

What is this song about?

In v. 2, the people sang God had become their salvation as the Egyptians were thrown into the sea. What does this say about their acknowledgement of God's hand in their exodus from Egypt?

Based on this song, what effect have the events at the Red Sea had on the inhabitants of Canaan? (vv. 13–18)

DISCUSSION: Why is it important to acknowledge God's hand in the events of our lives?

Bitter Water Made Sweet (vv. 22–27)

How long after the Red Sea does it take for the people to begin grumbling? What were they complaining about?

What promise did God make to them at Marah? Which of His names did He reveal here to the people?

Where did God lead the Israelites next?

Read John 4:1–14. How is the story of the bitter water from Exodus a picture of Jesus?

DISCUSSION: What do these passages tell us about trusting God for His provision in the wilderness?

DISCUSSION: How can we choose to believe more in the power of the God who has led us here vs. the reality of our circumstances?

Stories
FROM THE
Wilderness

WEEK 2 NOTES

Stories FROM THE Wilderness

WEEK 2 NOTES

HOW SHOULD I RESPOND?

What circumstances are you currently experiencing that may be a place where God is asking you to trust in Him?

Write a prayer praising God for who He is in this passage:

Because God is:

     I can:

Stories FROM THE Wilderness

TEACHING NOTES

Stories FROM THE Wilderness

TEACHING NOTES

Stories from the Wilderness

GROUP NOTES

Stories
FROM THE
Wilderness

GROUP NOTES

Stories from the Wilderness

WEEK 3

EXODUS 16
EXODUS 17

READ EXODUS 16

WHAT DOES THIS SAY?

Write a 2–3 sentence summary of this passage.

Who? What? Where? When?

List any repeated words or phrases.

List any transitional words.

WHAT DOES THIS SAY ABOUT GOD?

What characteristics of God do you see in this passage?

WHAT DOES THIS MEAN?

Bread from Heaven (Exodus 16)

What are the Israelites complaining about this time? To whom are they complaining?

What was God's response? (vv. 4–5)

What was God's purpose in sending food this way? (vv. 4 and 12)

When did the quail come?

When did the bread come?

What did the Israelites call the bread? Describe what it was like.

What happened when the Israelites measured their bread? (vv. 17–18)

DISCUSSION: What happened if the Israelites tried to save some for the next day? Why do you think God allowed this to happen?

What happened on the sixth day when the Israelites measured their manna? What was the response of the leaders? (vv. 22–26)

What happened to the leftover manna on the seventh day? (v. 24)

What did some of the Israelites do on the seventh day? (v. 27) How did God respond? (vv. 28–29)

DISCUSSION: Why do you think the idea of Sabbath was hard for the Israelites to grasp? What was their previous role/job in Egypt?

DISCUSSION: In light of this story in Exodus 16, what is the purpose of Sabbath?

How do we see God model Sabbath from the beginning of time? (See Genesis 2:1–3.)

Which day of creation did God create man? (Genesis 1:26–31) What did God do on the seventh day? Why do you think this is significant timing for man?

What did God ask Moses to do with some of the manna? (vv. 32–34) What does this tell us about ourselves?

Read Matthew 11:28–12:14. What does Jesus promise to those who come to Him? What day of the week did He say this? (Hint: 12:1)

DISCUSSION: Reading this passage in context, what do you think Jesus' message was saying about Sabbath?

Stories
FROM THE
Wilderness

WEEK 3 NOTES

READ EXODUS 17

WHAT DOES THIS SAY?

Write a 2–3 sentence summary of this passage.

Who? What? Where? When?

List any repeated words or phrases.

List any transitional words.

WHAT DOES THIS SAY ABOUT GOD?

What characteristics of God do you see in this passage?

WHAT DOES THIS MEAN?

Water from the Rock (Exodus 17:1–7)

What was Israel's complaint? To whom did they complain? Where have we seen this before?

When was the last time Moses stood on the Mountain of Horeb? (see Exodus 3:1–2) What is a nickname for this mountain according to Exodus 3:1?

DISCUSSION: Why is it significant that God provides water from a rock on Mount Horeb? What does this tell us about God?

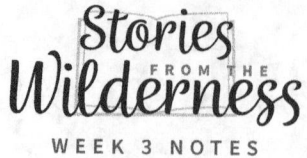
Read Psalm 78:1–32. What is the purpose of this Psalm?

What did the people really mean when they asked, "Can God really spread a table in the wilderness?" What was at the heart of their sin?

DISCUSSION: Why was it so important not to hide their failings of faith from future generations? How can we apply this in our own families?

Israel Defeats Amalek (Exodus 17:8–16)

Who are the Amalekites? (see Genesis 36:12) Knowing this, why do you think they would attack the Israelites? (See Genesis 27 for reference.)

70

What instruction does Moses give in v. 9? Whose staff does he hold?

What was Joshua's contribution to the fight? What was Moses'? How did Aaron and Hur contribute to the battle?

What did the staff represent to the people? What had it been used for up to this point? How had God already shown His miraculous power through this object? What confidence might the staff have given these people who have never seen battle?

What does Moses do to celebrate the victory? What name of God does Moses claim here? (v. 15)

DISCUSSION: The Hebrew name here is Yahweh Nissi. In war, a banner was a symbol of hope, victory, and/or a place to retreat. How is God our Yahweh Nissi today?

DISCUSSION: Read Colossians 4:12. How does Paul describe Epaphras? What does he do for the believers of the Colossian church?

The Greek word for *struggling* means "to endeavor with strenuous zeal, strife."[1] It's the same word used for a contest or fight. How does this give new meaning to what it means to pray for one another?

Who in your life comes alongside you to support you spiritually? Who are you coming alongside to support? As you close out this week, take some time to lift up someone God has placed in your life. Then text, call, or email them to let them know you are holding their arms up as they battle, struggling on their behalf.

1 Strong's Hebrew: 75. Agónizomai. *BibleHub.com*, biblehub.com/greek/75.htm.

Stories FROM THE Wilderness

WEEK 3 NOTES

Stories
FROM THE
Wilderness
WEEK 3 NOTES

HOW SHOULD I RESPOND?

The Hebrew word for *Sabbath* is "Shabbath" and means "to cease, to stop, to pause, to come to an end."[1] What does Sabbath look like today? What can we do to observe the Sabbath, not by law, but as an act of resting in Him for provision and restoration?

Write a prayer praising God for who He is in this passage.

Because God is:

    I can:

---

1 Strong's Hebrew: 7676. Shabbath. *BibleHub.com*. biblehub.com/hebrew/7676.htm

Stories FROM THE Wilderness

TEACHING NOTES

Stories FROM THE Wilderness

TEACHING NOTES

Stories from the Wilderness

GROUP NOTES

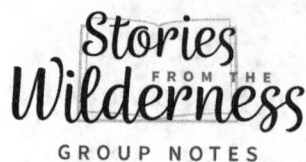

Stories *from the* Wilderness

GROUP NOTES

Stories from the Wilderness

WEEK 4

EXODUS 19
EXODUS 20
EXODUS 32

READ EXODUS 19-20

WHAT DOES THIS SAY?

Write a 2–3 sentence summary of this passage.

Who? What? Where? When?

List any repeated words or phrases.

List any transitional words.

WHAT DOES THIS SAY ABOUT GOD?

What characteristics of God do you see in this passage?

WHAT DOES THIS MEAN?

Israel at Mt. Sinai (Exodus 19)

Look up Mt. Sinai (either online or in a Bible concordance). What is another name for this mount? What other events take place here? Any other interesting facts?

What does God promise or "covenant" with Israel? (vv. 5–6)

How do the people answer God's covenant promise? (v. 8)

DISCUSSION: Look up the word *consecrate* in an English dictionary and write the definition.

DISCUSSION: Why was this process necessary before God could meet with the people? What does this tell us about God's character?

How does Moses describe the presence of God? (vv. 16–20)

The Ten Commandments (Exodus 20)
To whom does God give the Ten Commandments?

How does God "introduce" Himself in v. 2?

DISCUSSION: Our tendency with the Ten Commandments is to see them as a list of rules. But reading this passage in context of the covenant made in Exodus 19, what do these laws tell us about the character of God?

What did God command in vv. 22–26? What does this reveal about the character of God?

After God spoke, what was the immediate response of the people? What did they say? What did they do?

DISCUSSION: How did Moses' response differ? Why do you think his response was so different?

DISCUSSION: Read 1 Peter 2:1–10. How is the covenant made in Exodus 19–20 fulfilled through Jesus Christ?

READ EXODUS 32

WHAT DOES THIS SAY?

Write a 2–3 sentence summary of this passage.

Who? What? Where? When?

List any repeated words or phrases.

List any transitional words.

WHAT DOES THIS SAY ABOUT GOD?

What characteristics of God do you see in this passage?

WHAT DOES THIS MEAN?

The Golden Calf (Exodus 32)

How do the Israelites refer to Moses in v. 1? Why is this shocking?

What happened while Moses was on the mountain meeting with God? Whose idea was it?

Did this surprise you? Why or why not?

What does God say about the people to Moses? What does He say He is going to do?

What does Moses ask God to remember? And what does God do about it?

What did Moses do when he came down the mountain with Joshua?

What was Aaron's response to Moses' questioning in vv. 21–24?

DISCUSSION: What do vv. 25–30 tell us about sin? Moses goes back up the mountain and once again pleads with God. What did Moses ask? What is God's response? (vv. 30–35)

DISCUSSION: What does Exodus 32:34 tell you about God?

DISCUSSION: Moses said that the law was given to test the people. How quickly did the law reveal what was in their hearts and their ability to meet the condition?

Read the following verses. How is life under the law different from life in Christ?
John 1:16–17

Romans 8:1–17

Hebrews 12:18–29

DISCUSSION: Who is able to fulfill the condition of the covenant? Under this new covenant, what do we have?

Stories
FROM THE
Wilderness

WEEK 4 NOTES

Stories FROM THE Wilderness

WEEK 4 NOTES

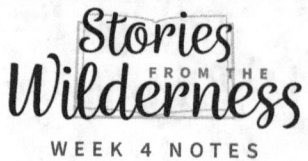
HOW SHOULD I RESPOND?

In light of this week's New Testament verses, how do we live out the law today? How should we "look different" than the world?

Write a prayer praising God for who He is in this passage.

Because God is:

    I can:

Stories FROM THE Wilderness

TEACHING NOTES

Stories FROM THE Wilderness

TEACHING NOTES

Stories FROM THE Wilderness

GROUP NOTES

Stories *from the* Wilderness

GROUP NOTES

Stories FROM THE Wilderness

WEEK 5

EXODUS 33
EXODUS 34
NUMBERS 9:15-23

READ EXODUS 33

WHAT DOES THIS SAY?

Write a 2–3 sentence summary of this passage.

Who? What? Where? When?

List any repeated words or phrases.

List any transitional words.

WHAT DOES THIS SAY ABOUT GOD?

What characteristics of God do you see in this passage?

WHAT DOES THIS MEAN?

The Command to Leave Sinai (Exodus 33:1–6)

What does God tell Moses to tell the people? How is this similar to what He has already said? How is this different?

What is the reaction of the people?

DISCUSSION: Why could God not go with them?

The Tent of Meeting (Exodus 33:7–11)

Where was the Tent of Meeting?

What would happen in the Tent?

What would happen with the cloud when Moses went to the Tent? What does this symbolize? (v. 9)

What would the people do in response? (vv. 8 and 10)

DISCUSSION: How does Moses speak to God? What does this tell us about the intimacy of a relationship with God?

Moses' Intercession (Exodus 33:12–23)

What does the word intercession mean?

What does Moses ask of God? (vv. 12–16)

How does God respond? (v. 17)

How does Moses respond? What does this tell us about his view of God? (v. 18)

How does God respond? (vv. 19–23)

DISCUSSION: List all of the attributes of God that He reveals to Moses in vv. 19–23. How does this help us understand His ways?

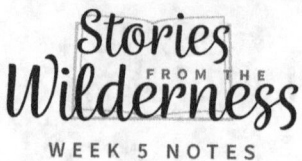
READ EXODUS 34

WHAT DOES THIS SAY?

Write a 2–3 sentence summary of this passage.

Who? What? Where? When?

List any repeated words or phrases.

List any transitional words.

WHAT DOES THIS SAY ABOUT GOD?

What characteristics of God do you see in this passage?

WHAT DOES THIS MEAN?

The Covenant Renewed (Exodus 34:1–27)

What does God tell Moses to do? Why?

How does God describe Himself?

How does Moses respond? (vv. 8–9)

DISCUSSION: When God reveals His character to us, how should we respond?

What does God tell Moses He will do? (v. 10)

What are the Israelites commanded to do? (vv. 11–26)

Which of His names does God reveal here?

DISCUSSION: What is the definition of *jealous*? What does it mean for God to be jealous?

DISCUSSION: What does the repetition of vv. 11–26 tell us about God? What does it reveal about our own hearts?

The Shining Face of Moses (Exodus 34:29–35)
What happened to Moses' face? Why?

How did the people respond?

READ NUMBERS 9:15–23

WHAT DOES THIS SAY?

Write a 2–3 sentence summary of this passage.

Who? What? Where? When?

List any repeated words or phrases.

List any transitional words.

WHAT DOES THIS SAY ABOUT GOD?

What characteristics of God do you see in this passage?

WHAT DOES THIS MEAN?

The Cloud Covering the Tabernacle (Numbers 9:15–23)

Read Exodus 25:8. Why does God command the people to build the Tabernacle? Where had His presence dwelled previously?

What is the pattern of action in these verses?

DISCUSSION: Think back to Exodus 13:17–22. How is God fulfilling that promise? What was required of the Israelites? What guides us today?

Read Hebrews 7:22–28. How is Jesus' intercession for us different from that of Moses and the priests in the Tabernacle?

Stories FROM THE Wilderness

WEEK 5 NOTES

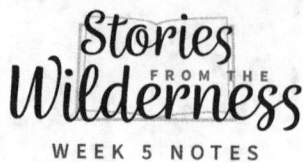

Stories FROM THE Wilderness

WEEK 5 NOTES

Stories from the Wilderness

WEEK 5 NOTES

HOW SHOULD I RESPOND?

Where have you seen God's glory on display in your life?

Write a prayer praising God for who He is in this passage.

Because God is:

     I can:

Stories FROM THE Wilderness

TEACHING NOTES

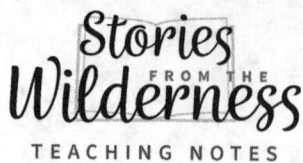

Stories
FROM THE
Wilderness

TEACHING NOTES

Stories FROM THE Wilderness

GROUP NOTES

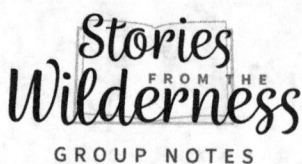

Stories
FROM THE
Wilderness
GROUP NOTES

Stories FROM THE Wilderness

WEEK 6

NUMBERS 13
NUMBERS 14

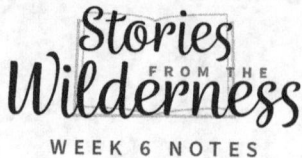
READ NUMBERS 13

WHAT DOES THIS SAY?

Write a 2–3 sentence summary of this passage.

Who? What? Where? When?

List any repeated words or phrases.

List any transitional words.

WHAT DOES THIS SAY ABOUT GOD?

What characteristics of God do you see in this passage?

WHAT DOES THIS MEAN?

Spies Sent Into Canaan (Numbers 13)
What did God instruct Moses to do? (vv. 1–2)

Who did Moses send as spies?

What eight instructions does Moses give the spies? (vv. 17–20)

What did the spies bring back with them?

What was positive about their report? What was negative?

Which six people groups did they report dwelt in the Promised Land? Where have we seen these names before?

How did the spies describe the descendants of Anak?

Who were the Amalekites descendants of (remember from Week 3)?

Read Genesis 10:6–20. Who are the remaining people groups descendants of?

Now read Genesis 9:18–29. What happened to the line of Canaan? How do we see this played out in Numbers 13?

DISCUSSION: What does this story tell us about the long-reaching effects of our sin and of our obedience?

DISCUSSION: Which spy spoke up in confidence? Why do you think he felt this way?

READ NUMBERS 14

WHAT DOES THIS SAY?

Write a 2–3 sentence summary of this passage.

Who? What? Where? When?

List any repeated words or phrases.

List any transitional words.

WHAT DOES THIS SAY ABOUT GOD?

What characteristics of God do you see in this passage?

WHAT DOES THIS MEAN?

The People Rebel (Numbers 14:1–12)

What was the people's response to the report? (vv. 1–4) What is one comment that goes a step further than we've seen before?

How was Caleb and Joshua's faith different from the other ten spies?

Look up *faithfulness* in a dictionary and write the definition.

DISCUSSION: What does it mean that God is faithful?

Think back on our study and read the following verses:

Exodus 6:6–9; Exodus 13:4–5; Exodus 13:11

Did the Israelites have a reason to doubt God's faithfulness? Why or why not?

Moses Intercedes for the People (Numbers 14:12–19)

What does Moses do for the people?

What is his argument for showing mercy to the Israelites?

What three characteristics of God does Moses quote? (vv. 17–18)

Where did God originally proclaim these characteristics to Moses? (Exodus 34:6–7)

God Promises Judgment (Numbers 14:20–38)
What is God's response to Moses' plea? What is the consequence of the sin of the Israelites?

Who will enter the Promised Land?

What happened to the ten spies?

Israel Defeated in Battle (Numbers 14:39–45)
How did the people respond to the consequence of their sin?

DISCUSSION: Why were the Israelites defeated? What does this teach us about trusting God and His Word?

DISCUSSION: Read Romans 4:13–25. What does this teach us about faith and believing God and His promises?

Stories
FROM THE
Wilderness

WEEK 6 NOTES

Stories
FROM THE
Wilderness

WEEK 6 NOTES

HOW SHOULD I RESPOND?

What is something God has promised that you struggle to believe? How does this passage reaffirm the faithfulness of God?

Write a prayer praising God for who He is in this passage.

Because God is:

I can:

Stories FROM THE Wilderness

TEACHING NOTES

Stories *from the* Wilderness

TEACHING NOTES

Stories FROM THE Wilderness

GROUP NOTES

Stories FROM THE Wilderness

GROUP NOTES

Stories from the Wilderness

WEEK 7

NUMBERS 20
NUMBERS 21

READ NUMBERS 20

WHAT DOES THIS SAY?

Write a 2–3 sentence summary of this passage.

Who? What? Where? When?

List any repeated words or phrases.

List any transitional words.

WHAT DOES THIS SAY ABOUT GOD?

What characteristics of God do you see in this passage?

WHAT DOES THIS MEAN?

The Waters of Meribah (Numbers 20:1–13)

What did God instruct Moses and Aaron to do? (v. 8) What did Moses do instead? (vv. 9–11)

DISCUSSION: Think back to Exodus 17. Why do you believe Moses would have behaved this way? What do Moses' actions reveal about the condition of his heart? In what ways can you relate to Moses?

What is God's response to Moses and Aaron? (v. 12)

What happened to Aaron? (Numbers 20:22–29)

DISCUSSION: Do you think the punishment matched the sin? What does God's response say about His character?

Read Psalm 95 and Hebrews 3:7–19.
What do the psalmist and the author of Hebrews call us to do?

DISCUSSION: How do we guard our hearts and continue to follow God daily even when we walk through the wilderness? Why is it necessary that we do this?

Edom Refuses Passage

Read Genesis 36:9. Who is the father of the Edomites? What do you remember of his story?

Read Deuteronomy 2:1–8. Why did God not permit the Israelites to go through Edom?

DISCUSSION: What does this teach us about God's provision even when His answer is no and we are still wandering in the wilderness?

READ NUMBERS 21

WHAT DOES THIS SAY?

Write a 2–3 sentence summary of this passage.

Who? What? Where? When?

List any repeated words or phrases.

List any transitional words.

WHAT DOES THIS SAY ABOUT GOD?

What characteristics of God do you see in this passage?

WHAT DOES THIS MEAN?

Arad Destroyed (Numbers 21:1–3)

What did the Israelites promise to do if God helped them defeat the Canaanites? What was the result? How did they respond?

The Bronze Serpent (Numbers 21: 4–9)

What prompted the Israelites to complain?

What did they call God's food? (v. 5)

How did God respond? (v. 6)

How did the people and Moses respond? (v. 7)

How did God provide salvation for the people of Israel? (vv. 8–9)

Read John 3:9–21. How does Jesus use this story to explain God's salvation?

DISCUSSION: How is the salvation Jesus gives better than the salvation of the bronze serpent?

The Song of the Well and the Defeat of King Sihon and King Og (Numbers 21:10–35)
How does God continue to provide in these passages?

How does God continue to guide in these passages?

How does God continue to keep His promises in these passages?

DISCUSSION: How does this shape our view of God and His character?

Stories
FROM THE
Wilderness

WEEK 7 NOTES

144

Stories FROM THE Wilderness

WEEK 7 NOTES

HOW SHOULD I RESPOND?

List the ways God has provided for you, guided you, and kept His promises to you.

Write a prayer praising God for who He is in this passage.

Because God is:

I can:

Stories FROM THE Wilderness

TEACHING NOTES

Stories FROM THE Wilderness

TEACHING NOTES

Stories from the Wilderness

GROUP NOTES

Stories FROM THE Wilderness
GROUP NOTES

150

Stories
FROM THE
Wilderness

WEEK 8

DEUTERONOMY 31
DEUTERONOMY 32
DEUTERONOMY 34

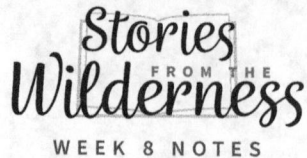
READ DEUTERONOMY 31

WHAT DOES THIS SAY?

Write a 2–3 sentence summary of this passage.

Who? What? Where? When?

List any repeated words or phrases.

List any transitional words.

WHAT DOES THIS SAY ABOUT GOD?

What characteristics of God do you see in this passage?

WHAT DOES THIS MEAN?

Joshua Commissioned to Succeed Moses (Deuteronomy 31)

What does Moses say to the Israelites in vv. 1–6?

What does Moses say to Joshua in vv. 7–8? Who is with them when he says this?

What does God say will happen to the people once they enter the Promised Land? (vv. 16 and 20)

What charge does God give Joshua in v. 23?

DISCUSSION: What is the purpose of the song of Moses? (vv. 19–21) What songs or Scripture verses do this for you today?

DISCUSSION: Why does Moses write the Book of the Law? (vv. 12–13) Read John 17:17. What is the result of hearing and learning God's Word based on these passages?

Stories
FROM THE
Wilderness
WEEK 8 NOTES

READ DEUTERONOMY 32

WHAT DOES THIS SAY?

Write a 2–3 sentence summary of this passage.

Who? What? Where? When?

List any repeated words or phrases.

List any transitional words.

WHAT DOES THIS SAY ABOUT GOD?

What characteristics of God do you see in this passage?

WHAT DOES THIS MEAN?

The Song of Moses (Deuteronomy 32)

What has God done for the Israelites throughout the wilderness?

How have the people responded?

What does God promise to do for His people even when they are unfaithful to Him?

What does Moses say to the people in vv. 44–47? How is this still true today?

What does God tell Moses in vv. 49–52? Why will he only see but not enter the Promised Land?

DISCUSSION: What does v. 51 teach us about the character of God and the way we represent Him to those around us?

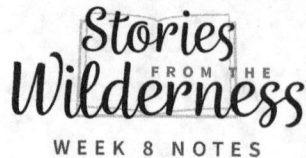
READ DEUTERONOMY 34

WHAT DOES THIS SAY?

Write a 2–3 sentence summary of this passage.

Who? What? Where? When?

List any repeated words or phrases.

List any transitional words.

WHAT DOES THIS SAY ABOUT GOD?

What characteristics of God do you see in this passage?

WHAT DOES THIS MEAN?

The Death of Moses (Deuteronomy 34)

How is Moses described in this passage?

Who buries Moses?

What does it mean that his "eye was undimmed and his vigor unabated"?

How is Joshua described in v. 9? What does this say about Moses as a leader?

Read Hebrews 11:23–29. How is Moses described in this passage?

Read Hebrews 3:1–6. How is Jesus greater than even Moses?

DISCUSSION: How can we be confident in our faith in Jesus Christ? How do we remain faithful to Him even when we are in the wilderness?

Stories
FROM THE
Wilderness

WEEK 8 NOTES

Stories

FROM THE

Wilderness

WEEK 8 NOTES

Stories from the Wilderness

WEEK 8 NOTES

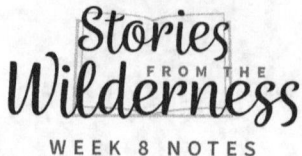
HOW SHOULD I RESPOND?

Write out 2–3 verses from Deuteronomy 32 that resonate with you and remind you who God is.

Write a prayer praising God for who He is in this passage.

Because God is:

    I can:

Stories *from the* Wilderness

TEACHING NOTES

Stories
FROM THE
Wilderness

TEACHING NOTES

Stories
FROM THE
Wilderness

GROUP NOTES

Stories from the Wilderness

GROUP NOTES

Stories from the Wilderness

WEEK 9

JOSHUA 1
JOSHUA 2

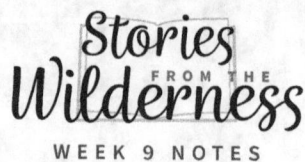
CONTEXT

Who wrote the book of Joshua?

What do you know about this author?

To whom was it written?

When was it written?

What is the genre of the book?

What was the intent or purpose?

What was going on in history when this book was written?

Stories FROM THE Wilderness

READ JOSHUA 1

WHAT DOES THIS SAY?

Write a 2–3 sentence summary of this passage.

Who? What? Where? When?

List any repeated words or phrases.

List any transitional words.

WHAT DOES THIS SAY ABOUT GOD?

What characteristics of God do you see in this passage?

WHAT DOES THIS MEAN?

God Commissions Joshua (Joshua 1)

How many times does God say "be strong and courageous"? How many times does He tell Joshua He will be with him?

What does God assure Joshua of that He had previously promised to Moses? What does this reveal to us about the nature of God? How far back does this covenant promise go?

DISCUSSION: In vv. 7–8, what does God tell Joshua to do? Why? What does that say about God's Word in our lives today?

How do the people respond to the command of Joshua? (vv. 16–18)

READ JOSHUA 2

WHAT DOES THIS SAY?

Write a 2–3 sentence summary of this passage.

Who? What? Where? When?

List any repeated words or phrases.

List any transitional words.

WHAT DOES THIS SAY ABOUT GOD?

What characteristics of God do you see in this passage?

WHAT DOES THIS MEAN?

Rahab Hides the Spies (Joshua 2)

How do you specifically see God fulfill in Chapter 2 what He promised in Chapter 1?

How did Rahab come to know about and believe in God? Why is it important to share our testimony with others? (Revelation 12:11)

DISCUSSION: What do vv. 17–19 tell us about safety when we walk in obedience within the boundaries of God's Word?

What is the response of the two spies? How is this different than the spies sent into Canaan in Numbers 13?

Read Joshua 6:22–25. How did Joshua uphold the promise the spies made to Rahab?

Read Matthew 1:1–6. What names do you recognize? Who was the mother of Boaz? What does this tell us about God?

DISCUSSION: When was a time you saw God go before you just as the spies witnessed through their encounter with Rahab?

Stories FROM THE Wilderness

WEEK 9 NOTES

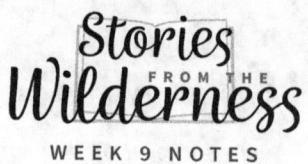

Stories from the Wilderness

WEEK 9 NOTES

HOW SHOULD I RESPOND?

Why are we able to be strong and courageous as God leads us even in the wilderness?

Write a prayer praising God for who He is in this passage.

Because God is:

I can:

Stories FROM THE Wilderness

TEACHING NOTES

Stories FROM THE Wilderness

TEACHING NOTES

Stories FROM THE Wilderness

GROUP NOTES

Stories
FROM THE
Wilderness
GROUP NOTES

Stories from the Wilderness

WEEK 10

JOSHUA 3
JOSHUA 4
JOSHUA 5

READ JOSHUA 3

WHAT DOES THIS SAY?

Write a 2–3 sentence summary of this passage.

Who? What? Where? When?

List any repeated words or phrases.

List any transitional words.

WHAT DOES THIS SAY ABOUT GOD?

What characteristics of God do you see in this passage?

WHAT DOES THIS MEAN?

Israel Crosses the Jordan (Joshua 3)

How did the people of Israel enter the wilderness in Exodus 14? How will they exit the wilderness?

What held back the waters of the Red Sea? (Exodus 14:21) What will hold back the waters of the Jordan River? (Joshua 3:13)

What was the condition of the Jordan River during this time of year? Why do you think Joshua included this detail? (v. 15)

What was the Ark of the Covenant? (See Exodus 25:10–22.) Why was it important that the priests carry it ahead of the people? Again, how do we see God fulfill the promises He made to Joshua in Chapter 1? What similar language do you see repeated here?

How will the people know God is with them? What confidence will that give them as they face the people groups currently living in the Promised Land?

The waters cut off from the city of _____ to _____ (which was 17 miles!). What do we call that sea today?

190

Stories FROM THE Wilderness

WEEK 10 NOTES

READ JOSHUA 4

WHAT DOES THIS SAY?

Write a 2–3 sentence summary of this passage.

Who? What? Where? When?

List any repeated words or phrases.

List any transitional words.

WHAT DOES THIS SAY ABOUT GOD?

What characteristics of God do you see in this passage?

WHAT DOES THIS MEAN?

Twelve Memorial Stones from the Jordan (Joshua 4)

What does God ask Joshua to do in vv. 1–7?

What was the purpose for building the altar?

DISCUSSION: Why was telling the next generation about God's might and power and faithfulness so important? Why do we still need to be doing this?

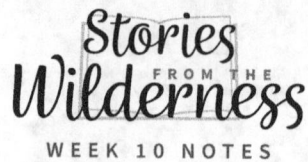
Write out vv. 23–24.

Read Hebrews 2:1 again. How do stones of remembrance help us today?

DISCUSSION: What stones of remembrance do you have in your own life?

Stories FROM THE Wilderness

WEEK 10 NOTES

READ JOSHUA 5:1–12

<u>WHAT DOES THIS SAY?</u>

Write a 2–3 sentence summary of this passage.

Who? What? Where? When?

List any repeated words or phrases.

List any transitional words.

WHAT DOES THIS SAY ABOUT GOD?

What characteristics of God do you see in this passage?

WHAT DOES THIS MEAN?

The New Generation is Circumcised (Joshua 5:1–9)

How do the kings respond to the Jordan River miracle? Where have we heard this before?

What did God command Joshua to do and why was this important? (vv. 2–9; see also Genesis 17:10–14, Exodus 12:48 and Deuteronomy 30:6)

What did the circumcision represent? (v. 9)

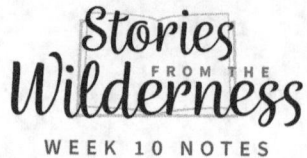
First Passover in Canaan (Joshua 5:10–12)

What did the Israelites celebrate while they were camped at Gilgal? What is the significance of celebrating this right after crossing into the Promised Land? (See Exodus 12:43–13:10.)

What other events signified the end to their wanderings in the wilderness? (v. 12)

Name everything you can think of from the time in the wilderness that is now gone. Name everything you can think of that is new about their new life in the Promised Land.

Read Revelation 21:1–7. Name the things of this earth that will one day be gone. What will be new? What will remain?

DISCUSSION: What hope does this give us as we walk through the wilderness?

Stories
FROM THE
Wilderness

WEEK 10 NOTES

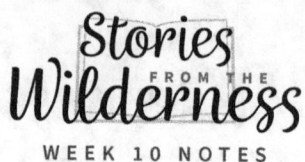

Stories FROM THE Wilderness

WEEK 10 NOTES

<u>HOW SHOULD I RESPOND?</u>

Which characteristics of God throughout this study have given you hope in your wilderness wandering?

Write a prayer praising God for who He is in this passage.

Because God is:

    I can:

Stories FROM THE Wilderness

TEACHING NOTES

Stories
FROM THE
Wilderness
GROUP NOTES

Stories
FROM THE
Wilderness
GROUP NOTES

Stories from the Wilderness

ADDITIONAL NOTES

Stories FROM THE Wilderness
ADDITIONAL NOTES

NAMES OF GOD	SCRIPTURE REFERENCE

MIRACLES IN THE WILDERNESS

Stories FROM THE Wilderness

ADDITIONAL NOTES

Stories
FROM THE Wilderness
ADDITIONAL NOTES

Stories FROM THE Wilderness

ADDITIONAL NOTES

feasting at the table

There's something magical about grilled cheese and tomato soup. It's a childhood staple, but over the last several years, it has become a popular grown-up meal as well. There are several grown-up tomato soup recipes out there, and this is my spin. By roasting the tomatoes, onions, and garlic beforehand, it adds a complex and slightly sweet flavor (without adding any extra sugar). Yes, I know it's easier to open a can, but I love the vibrance fresh roasted tomatoes provides.

For this recipe, I use a variety of tomatoes. I usually go with what looks best in the market that day: vine-ripened, plum, cherry, even grape tomatoes. I also do the extra step of removing the seeds. You can leave them in if you like, but the finished product will have a slightly bitter taste. It doesn't have to be four pounds exactly, but you want it to be close. For the onion, a sweet onion will yield a sweeter soup. A yellow onion will give you a more savory flavor. Play around and see which you like best. I also use a low-sodium broth. I like to control the amount of salt I cook with, so I often use low-sodium or no salt added products whenever possible. One of the other secrets to making this a flavorful soup is a process called *blooming the spices*. When you add the spices to hot oil and let them sauté for just a few seconds, it not only flavors the oil but also allows the natural flavors to come out of dried spices. It happens quickly, so be careful not to burn the spices. Otherwise, you will get a bitter flavor.

I love serving this alongside a yummy grilled cheese. I typically love a sharp white cheddar on fresh baked bread. The sharpness is a nice contrast to the roasted sweetness of this soup. For a low-carb option, serve with a small green salad. It's a delicious and mostly healthy lunch. Enjoy!

213

ERIN'S ROASTED TOMATO SOUP

Time: 60 min
Yield: 4–6 Servings

INGREDIENTS

4 pounds fresh tomatoes (mixed varieties: plum, vine-ripened, cherry, or grape tomatoes)
1 sweet or yellow onion
6–8 garlic cloves
kosher salt
fresh ground pepper

2 tablespoons extra virgin olive oil
2 teaspoons thyme
1 teaspoon basil
a dash of red pepper flakes (you can add more if you prefer soup with a kick)
1 cup low sodium vegetable or chicken broth

INSTRUCTIONS

1. Preheat the oven to 425 degrees.
2. Remove the seeds from the larger tomatoes and cut in half.
3. Rough chop the onion (you want larger pieces so they don't burn).
4. Crush the garlic and remove the paper.
5. Place the tomatoes, onions, and garlic on a sheet pan. Drizzle with 1–2 tablespoons of extra virgin olive oil, 2 teaspoons of salt, and some fresh ground pepper.
6. Roast at 425 degrees for about 35–45 minutes or until the edges of onion brown and tomatoes shrivel and begin to brown. Remove from oven and set aside.
7. In a heavy bottom pot or dutch oven, heat 1 tablespoon extra virgin olive oil over medium heat. Add red pepper flakes, thyme, and basil. Sauté for about one minute.
8. Add the roasted tomatoes, onion, garlic, and juices to the pot. Add 1 cup of broth.
9. Bring to a boil and simmer for about 5 minutes.
10. Using an immersion blender, blend the soup until smooth.*
11. Add 1 teaspoon kosher salt and a few cracks of fresh ground pepper. (You can add more salt if needed).
12. Serve with grilled cheese sandwiches for a little nostalgia!

*Depending on how much juice you get from the roasted tomatoes, you may need to add more broth to get the desired consistency.

NOTE: If you do not have an immersion blender, you can transfer the soup (carefully!) to a food processor or blender. Blend until smooth then return to the pot.

about Erin

ERIN H. WARREN is passionate about equipping and encouraging women to discover God's truths for themselves. She is the author of *Feasting on Truth: Savor the Life-giving Word of God*, leads and teaches Bible study through her ministry Feasting on Truth, and has published several Bible studies. She and her husband, Kris, have three littles (who aren't so little anymore), and they live in Central Florida. She loves a house full of people and a table full of food and hopes tacos never go out of style. You can find more information about Feasting on Truth on her website: FeastingOnTruth.com. You can also connect with her on Instagram: @erinhwarren and @feastingontruth and YouTube: www.youtube.com/c/erinhwarren.

216

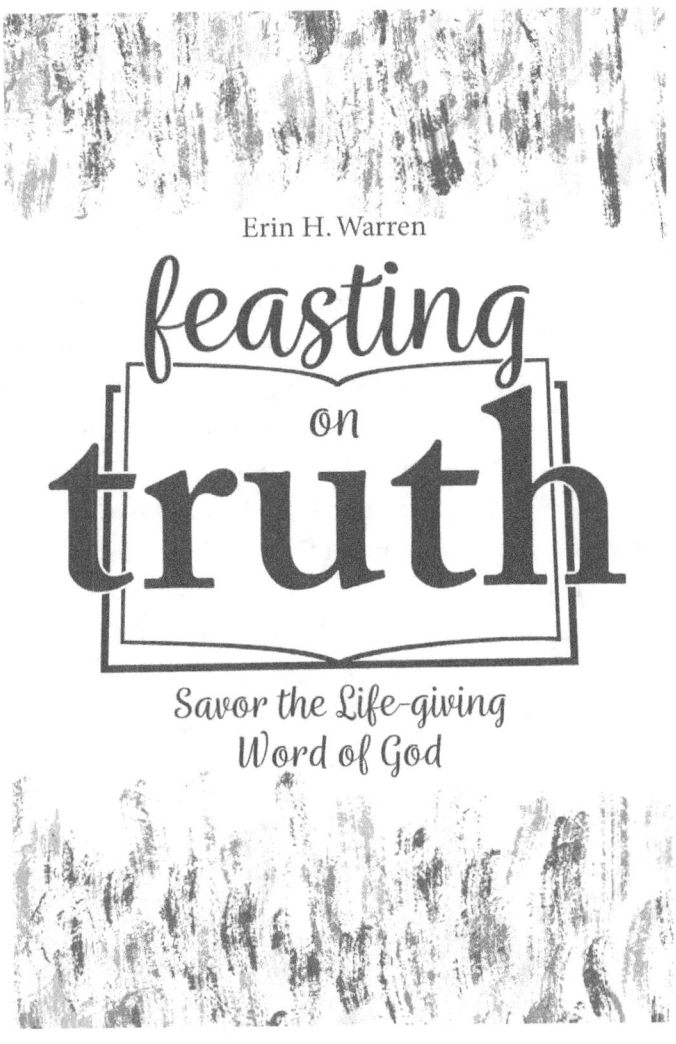

Erin H. Warren

feasting on truth

Savor the Life-giving
Word of God

FEASTING ON TRUTH
SAVOR THE LIFE-GIVING WORD OF GOD

The Word of God is our very life, but Erin Warren felt anything but alive. Her husband was sick. Her world was falling apart, and she had questions. Feel-good faith was not enough; she needed deep, sustaining truths.

Through her own wrestling, Erin Warren addresses the obstacles that held her back when it came to Bible study and how she discovered to savor the life-giving Word of God.

The word *feast* is rooted in abundance. That is what awaits us in the pages of Scripture: a table laid out before us, not only for our essential nourishment, but for our enjoyment.

FeastingOnTruth.com/Books

TO DWELL IN OUR MIDST

A STUDY OF THE TABERNACLE AND HOW IT POINTS US TO JESUS

Why study this ancient tent? What does knowing about the Tabernacle have to do with our faith on this side of the cross? Everything. This tent is not merely ritual or history or good information—it's essential to understanding our salvation. Our detailed and deliberate God gave us the Tabernacle because one day, He would give us Jesus. It's an invitation into a relationship with our Holy God. Discover God's plan to dwell in our midst through Jesus Christ.

FeastingOnTruth.com/Dwell

LIGHT & LIFE

AN INDUCTIVE STUDY ON PSALM 119

We hear it all the time: we need to read the Bible every day. But why is it so important that we know, understand, and apply this ancient book to our lives today? What's in it for us? In Psalm 119, we see over and over that God's Word brings life, and it's a light to guide us. If we truly knew the power the Word of God has in our lives, we wouldn't be able to put it down.

FeastingOnTruth.com/LightAndLife